Farting Cows

Published by Upgraded Books

Thank you so much for choosing my coloring book! Your support means the world to me.

I am the founder of Upgraded Books -- a small business dedicated to bringing calm and joy to the world through books. :)

Every purchase and every colorful page really brightens my day and I would love to share my other labors of love with you!

Whether you're in need of relaxation, seeking inspiration, or simply craving a good laugh, I have a coloring book that matches your mood.

Love,
Simone

This Belongs To

_____

www.ingramcontent.com/pod-product-compliance
Lightning Source LLC
Chambersburg PA
CBHW080427030426
42335CB00020B/2630